Building the Energetic Immune System Healing for Empaths and empathic children

April Walker

Cover Art:
by 30Ashley Josephine Foreman
https://www.thirteentwentystudios.com

Cover Design & Illustrations: Sara Donato

Formatting Graphics:

For information or questions contact: www.aprilwalker.com

"This sacred book will eliminate the the statement "I feel too much." There is no such thing. Feeling is the ultimate blessing and having a guidebook like this is essential for managing a deeply lived and felt life. Thank you, April. This was the missing link."

—Robert Sturman, Photographer/Artist

"In my practice, I have worked with many Empaths. They typically are very sensitive to feelings, emotions, pain and joys of others and it can come at a cost— because they are sensitive to other people's energies, they can be energetically overwhelmed. They can expend too much of their own energies and they often do not know if pain, misery, negative energy and emotions are theirs or someone else's. When an empath gets into a large crowd of people, it can be like they just ran a marathon and they must take steps to recuperate. They can become reclusive and avoid being around people. If empaths learn to manage their own energy, it can be helpful. Otherwise they will often avoid friends and loved ones for fear of throwing them into illness, and may have guilt because of that factor.

Something else less talked about is that they tend to be sensitive to chemicals, bioenergetic fields and a list of other things. Many of them have allergies. Their sympathetic nervous systems can be kicked into overdrive easily. Therefore things that nourish and support parasympathetic systems are very important for empaths such as rest, recuperation, sleep, nutritious food, meditation of various forms, chi gong, yoga and prayer. Empaths have a broader lens with a more in-depth view of reality. Many of them are aware of unseen energies, beings, those who have passed on, and more. They can be susceptible to these energies and they can have nightmarish experiences. The veil between these realms is very thin for these folks. Because they are few and far between, many times empaths are viewed as odd or crazy, but they are not.

The Bible discusses gifts of the spirit. Gifts differ and are meant to help each other, but they need to be understood, managed and used wisely. I believe empaths have a spiritual gift.

Empaths have a unique ability to help people that others can't. If they are aware of how to take care of themselves and how to be strong, healthy individuals, then they do not have to be so affected by the storms of pain and emotions that come flying at them. Empaths are susceptible to the reality of good and evil influences at play. They have to make extraordinary effort to stay in the light. Dark energies unseen by most can be addictive which allows them more power and freedom, and that can be toxic on all levels. This dark influence happens to everyone. Empaths are just more susceptible. Everyone is capable of these things, however for empaths it is a natural ability, like an artist. Some artists from a young age can create amazing art without a lot of work, empaths' gifts are very similar.

April's book offers awareness and tools that will help empaths to find balance and well being."

—Dr. Ralph Jeffery, DC

Acknowledgements

This book is dedicated to Karen Canto, my introverted empathic friend. Karen was my first Reiki teacher. She taught me to trust in my gifts and encouraged me to pursue them. Because of her, I opened my Reiki practice.

I also dedicate this book to the many empathic students and clients who continued asking similar questions that make up the basis of what is written in these pages. Without Karen, my students, and clients, this book would not have been possible.

Thank you to my loving family for their support with this and many other projects.

My personal gratitude to Dana Lee, an amazing friend, who provided boundless support and help with the initial draft reviews. Additional thanks to Kimberly Spina, Kelly Darpinian, Clare Conrotto, Roxanne Scoggins and Martina Vogt whose left-brained organization of my right-brained way of being made this book possible.

About the Author

April Walker, MA is an internationally recognized Master Healer, Mentor, and Life Wellness Coach. As an intuitive empath known for her transformative healing experiences, educational mentorship programs, and interactive coaching style, April has helped healers and empaths around the world live more balanced, happy lives.

April Walker and her family live in Central California, together with eight goats, two dogs, and two cats.

As a professor and Integrative Energy Therapist, April has mentored, trained, and worked compassionately alongside thousands of people, and a great many of them have been empaths. Many are employed in the service of others: physicians, health care workers, managers, administrative support staff, first responders, veterinarians, yoga teachers, photographers, writers, parents, and healers.

Helping others to experience less suffering is April's life passion. April helps empaths clear debilitating emotional baggage, release limiting beliefs, identify authentically with who they really are, and courageously lead more balanced, satisfying lives. "Healing for Empaths" is a work of the heart dedicated to all sensitive souls.

Table of Contents

1

Introduction

As an intuitive empath myself, I have had to allow myself to feel, know, and profoundly accept who I am. Feeling too much for others as well as oneself can be debilitating. Learning how to feel and heal my own empathic imbalances as well as helping others in a way that edifies all parties is the crux of this book. Like so many empaths, unconsciously acquiring the emotional and physical suffering of others was a self-destructive and unsustainable practice that I was unaware of. In the past, helping others to find healing and comfort came at my personal expense.

I absorbed the suffering of others at an emotional and physical level, which depleted my vitality rather than offering true healing. Over the years I have developed an energetic toolbox of practices that can bring balanced, lasting healing for all empaths. My intention is to help you live a more balanced and joyful life being an empath. It is each individuals journey to find out what tools work best for them. It is not my intention that an empath be constantly protecting themselves and shielding, this would promote fear and that goes against an empaths very nature of being open and seeking joy. This book contains targeted exercises and real-life examples that are designed to help you steadily grow in capacity, appreciation and application of your unique empathic gifts.

The exercises are meant to assist a person in first recognizing their own energy and then to recognize what belongs to someone else. The intention is not that you walk around constantly bubbling yourself and doing exercises - it is that you learn to determine what is actually your responsibility and then how to raise and balance your energy for your wellbeing. Empaths need to understand the depth of power present within their intentions and how healthy energy boundaries are best for everyone.

What is the Energetic Immune System?

Just as our physical immune system defends us against bacteria, viruses, and other potentially harmful foreign bodies, our energetic immune system protects us from negative thoughts, emotions, intentions, and other energies that do not belong to us and can impair our physical and emotional well-being.

"It is my hope that this book, gleaned from the work of a lifetime, will help to guide you or the empathic person in your life out of suffering and into lasting wellness, balance, and joy."

—April Walker

"Energy is all there is."

—Albert Einstein

2

What Is an Empath and Why Do We Know So Little About It?

The word empath is derived from the Greek em "in" and pathos "feeling" and means "able to feel otherness." Empaths have the ability to tune into energetic fields on various planes of existence and possess a magnified sensitivity to prana, or the energies of life. This may include life energies beyond the human form such as animals and plant life.

Empathic gifts tend to be genetic, passed along through bloodlines. My experience is that people are created and born as empaths, similar to being born with blue or brown eyes. Some particular gifts skip generations like any other inherited trait.

Others are created through circumstance or happenings such as trauma, codependency, narcissistic parent(s) which can lead to their energetic fields becoming worn and tattered, eventually causing holes.

empath/*noun*

(chiefly in science fiction) *a person with the paranormal ability to apprehend the mental or emotional state of another individual.*

Empaths are highly sensitive individuals with a magnified ability to detect and appropriate emotional imbalances similar to the physical body's dynamic interaction with various states of illness and disease. Many empaths can become so blended and entangled in the energies of others that they are unaware that what they are feeling is not their own emotion. It helps to think of it as an energetic melding.

This may be due in part to increased or stronger activation of mirror neurons in sensitive people, though more scientific research is needed. I have found that the challenge lies with the subconscious mind, which absorbs more energies and information rather than allowing them to pass through.

"My work is about emotions for which I have no words"

—Robert Sturman, Artist, Photographer

There are many levels of empathic sensitivities, as I have learned through my practice in helping people to clear negative emotions and limiting beliefs. Frequently, kinesthetic muscle testing reveals the underlying seeds of suffering and helps the body reveal information about what needs healing. Many times, something needs to be remembered or connected with from the past that is still affecting health and happiness in the present moment.

A clear sign that someone is an empath is that they are holding on to the experiences of others dating back to early childhood. For example, it is not unusual to uncover negative trapped emotions from early life personally belonging to the empath as well as more trapped emotions belonging to other people from that timeframe. There is no fault to be assigned to anyone for this. The reality of an empath is that he or she conduits multiple signals across many wavelengths, with emotional input streaming into their senses continually throughout life. Without proper training, understanding and self-care, empaths can easily become a heavy sponge for the emotions, experience, chronic stress, and illnesses of others.

Personally, I was at the level of what might be called an extreme empath. I had acquired so many emotional states from others that I had trouble knowing what my true feelings were about anything. Particularly my experiences of mint chip ice cream and also shopping with friends illustrate this perfectly. As a child, I used to love going to the local ice cream shop with my mother to get mint chip ice cream cones. Alongside my mom, I could not wait to taste the cold refreshing ice cream. Together we would savor every creamy green chocolate-speckled bite, grinning the entire time. Yet, on my own or with friends, I really did not like mint chip ice cream and wondered how I could ever have eaten it, until the next time I went to the ice cream shop with my mother. Whenever she was involved, mint chip ice cream tasted like pure heaven. I wondered what was wrong with me that I could feel such a dramatic difference from one outing to the next.

This emotional appropriation pattern continued into my young adulthood. When shopping with friends for clothing I would find so many perfect outfits only later to wonder why I had purchased clothing that was so clearly suited to what my friend liked and not at all my style. In fact, shopping with friends often resulted in purchasing items that I would never wear. Learning to identify my true feelings was a deep mystery wrought with confusion and pain.

Even more mysterious and dangerous to me as an extreme level empath was the propensity to transmute, or take on, the physical illnesses as well as the emotional baggage of others.

This unfortunate practice threatened threatened my very survival since in my practice (pls. see comment about re: professional career framework) I often work with patients suffering from serious chronic diseases.

For example, someone would have a headache, spend a little time with me and then leave feeling much better. I would be left with their headache. Some empaths transmute illnesses and also emotional signals from others.

Imagine being in a professional work environment and knowing when someone is lying or manipulating another person into taking on more work. You can see why this may cause anxiety. Even if no one had verbalized it, this knowing would cause discomfort. In my case, my health and the health of my child were in serious trouble before I finally figured out this "empathing" thing. Learning to build sustainable empathic boundaries and energetic immunity is critical.

Empaths throughout the ages have been gifted with additional ways of knowing. There have been times in history that energetic gifts of detection and healing have led to physical danger and persecution for empaths. Our culture has a history of shaming those who appear dramatic or different, up to and including persecution, marginalization and even death. Living outside of society's norms often has a high price. Minimally, an empathic person may appear to be moody. Parents might seek to protect a sensitive child, discouraging all forms of anything that looks different to keep their child safe from harm.

In today's culture, parents may try to "toughen up" their child to help them make it in a perilous world. Many times the parent is an empath himself and has suffered because of it. He may want to tamp down the gifts he has passed on to his children to spare them the sorrow of feeling so much. We live in a world that numbs sensations of being and such avoidance can only lead to more suffering. This is why we know so little about what is at its essence a divine gift.

Some empaths are aware of multidimensional space and time. They may sense other realms, beings and energies like nature spirits, ancestors and so on. They may be aware on some level of lower and/or higher energy fields. This is another reason why clearing practices and energy management are vitally important. These tools are illuminated in rich detail in upcoming chapters. Empaths are soulful, not necessarily subscribing to a specific religion, but they feel drawn to nurture their soul, and prioritize connection with nature energies. They may pray to the divine for help in protecting themselves. Whether they realize it or not, empaths interact with guidance from a Divine source, such as angels or ascended relatives.

Why pray to the Divine? Simply put, because it works. Empaths are already who they are. This soulful awareness brings all prana into balance for them.

Ideally, if empaths learn to love themselves, and chooses not to absorb the negative emotions and limited beliefs wafting from the emotions and thoughts of others. Confusion can come from not recognizing who they are and how to harness their particular pranic sensitivities. Empaths benefit from learning to sense subtle energies and understand the role of chakras and other energy fields. Many people are uncomfortable with the esoteric nature of empathic gifts.

Our society holds the belief that esoteric gifts are not real, meaningful, or natural in the hands of lay people. But that is who empaths are. Empathic gifts do not just belong to a select few garbed in religious vestments locked behind gilded doors. Empaths sense the world around them as variant energies and are happiest when they are free to do so.

Their joy is expanded to help heal the world when gifts are allowed to blossom and grow. The sooner empaths learn to work in communion with their energy, the happier and healthier we will all be. Growing up in a home full of love and support can make all the difference in the world. Being raised in a violent and abusive home without proper self-care and nurturing from parents will dramatically affect an empath's health and well-being, particularly due to their high level of sensitivities and absorption patterns.

Am I an Empath?

Take a few minutes to answer the questions below to determine if you could benefit from building a stronger empathic immunity.

- ✓ Have you ever been told that you are "too sensitive" or "too emotional"?

- ✓ Have you been told you were "moody"?

- ✓ Are you easily overwhelmed or do you often feel anxious, fatigued, or drained in crowds of people?

- ✓ Do you seem to have a "knowing" about what others are feeling?

- ✓ Do you seem to know when other people are lying or faking it?

- ✓ Do you prefer the mountains or ocean over the city?

- ✓ Were you frequently ill as a child?

- ✓ Do you have trouble with boundaries? Trouble saying no to others when it is in your best interest to do so, especially if they will be upset by your saying no?

- ✓ Do you love nature and animals?

- ✓ Do you find that you are the peacemaker, the good listener and often the dumping ground for others to vent to?

- ✓ Does clutter contribute to feeling overwhelmed?

- ✓ Are you an "ideas" person, an outside the box thinker who is good at easily identifying another person's best attributes for them?

- ✓ Do you find yourself always helping the underdog?

- ✓ Are you sensitive to violent movies or movies reflecting emotional pain?

- ✓ Do you find that you are more tired than you "should" be, that even sleep does not help?

- ✓ Do you find that you have a need for solitude?

- ✓ Do you have digestive disorders?

✓ Do you hate conflict and avoid it at all cost?

✓ Do you try to fix others or fix things for others? "I must have done something wrong, how can I fix it?"

✓ Does it seem that sometimes other people are easily offended or threatened by you without an obvious reason?

Points (one per check mark)

0 – 2	You are probably not an empath.
2 – 5	It is likely that you are an empath.
6 – 8	You are an empath.
9 or more	You are a very strong empath.

Exercise 1 - Self-Reflection

When in your life have you experienced the confusion of feelings, physical ailments, or preferences of others rather than your own? Can you think of a few examples that stand out in your life when you now recognize you were empathing?

3

Building the Empathic Immune System and Why You Must Take Responsibility

Now that the reality of your empathic gifts has been revealed, it's time to cultivate healing and protection around your unique set of abilities. Recognizing that a person actually is an empath is the important first step. Outside of a trauma experience, which requires special attention and healing, no one can make you feel anything. Therefore, you have more control over your emotions than you think. We allow others to adversely affect our mood.

We replay the tapes in our mind of old programming, repeating the messages over again and again, locked in a stale dance of disquiet. Lack of understanding and a disconnect within ourselves keep us on this frustrating path.

Deep layers form grooves upon grooves of negative programming that wind throughout our lives masquerading as truth. But it's not our truth. Our truth is born of light. Learn to tune in to know ourselves, connect to our own feelings and natural state so that we can turn the key to knowing when an outside influence suddenly enters our field. We can take full responsibility for how we feel and begin to live fully in the light in the present moment—body, mind, and soul.

Take responsibility for healing through clarification

Take full responsibility for your empathic reality. Do not assume that all emotions you're feeling are yours. Remember that your sensitivities often detect a collective of the energetic spectrum and that for you, a simple pause to consider the source of these emotions is a very healthy and effective practice. When you're with a person, and you're confused by your feelings at that moment, ask them to clarify their own mood before assuming that you are the center or owner of these emotions.

Begin to encourage a healthy pause by thinking or saying, "Did I do or say something wrong? "The person may tell you what they are actually feeling, rather than assuming that you just know, and it may not be related to you at all.

Communication is a powerful thing. People may not always tell you the truth due to conflict avoidance or a lack of practice with open communications, but empaths will feel a subtle shift by just asking the questions and allowing time to consider that not all "feelings" are their own.

The key is tuning in inwardly instead of turning in outwardly. Learn to recognize when you are not in a high vibration and do something about it immediately. Then take steps to raise your energy vibration. Using the clearing and protection tools in this book will assist you in protecting your empathic immune system. Stop feeling the energy of others 24 hours a day just because you can. Instead of always tuning into others as a distraction from your own life, learn to work on your own challenges to deepen your experience of life. Turn your skill in empathizing toward yourself. Identify when you are feeling the internal conflict with what others believe. Instead of tuning into how they feel and adopting their sentiment, try identifying how you actually feel about the subject and perhaps state that you do not actually feel the same way. At least do so in your head if the situation does not allow you to voice your truth and feel the freedom.

Prior to understanding who we are, we may have a tendency to assume responsibility for the emotions and problems of those in our environment. We must gain the understanding of what is ours and what is theirs. We must come to the liberating realization that solving everything for everyone does not help them learn their own lessons and in fact robs them of the blessings of self-realization.

Healing any and all codependent tendencies is a top priority for empaths who so often extract self-value through helping others. Separate any need to be valued from the fact that every human being has intrinsic value. Learn to value yourself outside of what you can do for others. It is better to focus your abilities on allowing others to find their own way. It is a deeper and more lasting joy to allow ourselves to savor life without so much external input.

Step into your unique authenticity with courage and joy. When you open the door to your genuine self, you are truly free. Your pure vibration lifts the energy of all beings around you. When you are yourself, there is no reason to hide who you are. It is empowering to be exactly yourself at all times, no matter what others think. If you have habitually hidden who you are in order to make yourself or others feel more comfortable, you are wasting time. Invest in your happiness and the power of your divine gifts by creating a vibration of trust through authentic interactions.

Leaning in to who you are means acknowledging when you are uncomfortable and doing something about it. "I am" uncomfortable then taking steps to take care of your needs This means if you are irritated by bright lights, being willing to put sunglasses on even if you are inside. It means speaking your truth even if it looks different. Letting go of what others think and focusing on what you need.

"I have learned that if you face trials head on, you can find more strength. Don't run away from what looks like a challenge. It may be an important part of your path. You have to be persistent and follow what you believe."

—Tao Porchon-Lynch, Dancing Light: "The Spiritual Side of Being Through the Eyes of a Modern Yoga Master"

4

The Silver Lining

The world needs us. Empaths are amazingly gifted individuals with a great capacity to see the goodness in people, to add balance and to heal. Not all empathing experiences are a struggle. Once a highly sensitive individual truly realizes his or her authentic self and has fortified personal emotional and experiential immunity, space to witness the unfolding of one's divine dharma has been created. The silver lining of one's life purpose and natural gifts is revealed.

Empaths can experience deep bliss and enjoy that feeling more intensely than other people. They can understand how to help others because they are more intuitive and have more knowing of how to help. Empaths are amazing listeners. They can communicate "what it feels like" and in doing so assist someone in healing. They have the gift of sensing and tune in to where the issue is for someone quickly and effectively.

An empath is often unconsciously influenced by the desires, thoughts and moods of others. They can feel physical sensitivities. They may even experience illness and fatigue based on the emotions of others in their environment. They often serve as a mirror, reflecting what needs to be healed for someone else. Instead of feeling burdened from being an empath, learn to embrace it.

Empaths are capable of consciously resonating higher frequencies out into the world, and thereby amplifying the vibrations of those around us. Often, we can alter the mood, health or wellbeing of another through the use of our gifts. The intention of an empath is a powerful thing. Focus on something amazing you have experienced in your life, a high frequency place or a happy memory, with the intention of sharing it with others. It could be a positive feeling you experienced such as how you felt after a good yoga session, or after hearing the musical laughter of a blissful toddler.

Use that positive energy to fill your body, mind, and spirit then imagine that energy filling your current environment. Visualize and intend your energy expanding from your heart, feel the expansion energy pushing out as though you could knock something over. Use this energy to overcome issues with relationships and past negative situations that perhaps left you feeling unloved and unappreciated.

Empaths are often psychic in some way; they are skilled human lie detectors. They often:

- Give really accurate advice.

- Can sense dangerous energy.

- Avoid harm by trusting their intuition.

- Are incredibly creative.

- Are natural problem solvers—they have the ability to tap into universal knowledge to find answers, often without knowing it.

- Attract people naturally due to their nonjudgmental nature.

- Make people feel better just through the quality of their presence.

- Have an enhanced ability to problem solve by emotionally connecting with others.

- Are incredible at clearing negative energy at the office, home, and any public and private spaces.

As an Empath: What's in It for Me?

- Trust your gut and waste less time: If something feels "off," it most likely is off. We can begin to address things sooner because that knowing/sensing lets us know.

- We have the ability to "tune in" more deeply to the energies that we love and enjoy, far more than the average "muggle". Overall, we can feel more joy.

- We can actually tune into a person's energy, voice, skillset, or knowledge and acquire some of that information or even a skillset.

- Empaths may experience a sense of danger before an event happens. If an empath is in danger, they often have a way of being able to connect with the dangerous person and may be able to find their way out of danger.

- Magic happens around empaths! Synchronicities, special and fun experiences, that others may categorize as coincidences.

- Empathic superpowers are: keen intuition, sensing abilities, the ability to connect with all types of people. Some empaths can even pick up on another language very quickly.

"We are speaking to the world around us in every moment of every day through a language that has no words."

—Richard Gordon, Quantum Touch

5

Types of Empaths

Not all empaths are the same. Some are introverted and some are extroverted. They can hold various degrees of energy discernment and all benefit from learning energy balance skills. A person may be one or a combination of the following types of empaths:

Emotional - This is the most common type of empath. They have the ability to pick up on the emotions of others. They will know that someone is sad even if he is smiling, acting happy, and saying he is happy. This may be just a knowing or the emotional empath may feel the other person's emotions as if they were his own.

Geomantic - Those who are affected by the electromagnetic field of the earth. They may feel very happy in particular places. They may also be sensitive to highly energetic places such as Sedona, Arizona; sacred places; churches and stones. They may be sensitive to the history of a place or an item, and can experience anxiety, headaches, or nausea before natural disasters on the planet or when something tragic has happened in an area. They often feel sadness when the earth is negatively affected.

Animal - Many empaths feel connected to the emotions and needs of animals. They may have the gift of animal communication.

Plant - A plant empath has a knowing about what a plant needs and may glean information from trees and plants. They may even feel compelled to buy a plant that is dying in order to save it. They are often labeled a "green thumb."

Intuitive – An intuitive empath may pick up on information simply by sharing space with another person. He can see beyond the emotions of others, often understanding at a deeper level why someone may feel a particular way. He has the ability to help others know themselves more fully. Intuitive empaths also tend to give good advice.

Kinesthetic – A kinesthetic empath feels information in her body. She or he feels the pain and discomfort of others as if they were his or her own. She or he may pick up on the symptoms and ailments of others, which means they may experience indicators of someone else's pain or illness in his or her own physical body. Some may be able to transmute and transform the illnesses of others. It is important for Kinesthetic Empaths to become aware of this ability, and to focus their intention only on the indicator or knowledge to be accepted but not take on the full energy of the issue. Transmuting needs a strong immune system, clarity of self and energetic daily practices to maintain health. In today's culture and environments, transmuting is not recommended.

Medium – This empath has the ability to see, hear, or feel, or a combination of these from spirits and those who have passed away.

Psychometric – A psychometric empath has the ability to pick up information from inanimate objects, such as stuffed animals, photographs, buildings, automobiles, etc.

Precognitive – Precognitive empaths feel or know occurrences before they happen. They may experience dread, anxiety, or other symptoms of great apprehension or fear.

Telepathic – Someone who is a telepathic empath has the ability to read the unexpressed thoughts of others.

Claircognizant – A claircognizant empath experiences a clear, natural knowing if something needs to be done. For instance, she may receive intuitive information that allows her to solve a problem quickly. She may even pick up on a skill set or knowledge from someone just by listening to him, tuning into the sound of his voice, his passion for a topic, and his energy.

Intellectual – This empath may have a knowing about another person's ideas and perspectives. They may even pick up on verbal accents and foreign languages remarkably quickly.

Crystal and stone – Crystal and stone empaths experience knowing about the qualities of crystals, gemstones, and rocks and how these stones may be helpful to themselves and others.

6

Shielding and Protecting

It is important that empaths not live closed down and in fear. Please understand that these particular tools are only for use now and again like in the beginning of your journey or when you have been extra stressed. Constantly feeling that they have to do cleansing and protection rituals every day to be "safe" implies danger and promotes a fear state and that goes against their open natural way of being.

The first step is to become deeply self-aware. Know how you feel. Step out of victim entrapment patterns and into who you are. Raise your own vibration. Become bigger energetically, not smaller. Decide to stop allowing outside influences in. Take responsibility. Take steps to deal with issues from your past. Practice tuning-in every chance you get. Do not stay in fear. Observe, and take positive steps to overcome the issues that are holding you back from tuning in to you.

When in doubt, tune inward! The best advice is to have good boundaries and learn to say no, without explanation. Be authentically you and ask for what you need. Become a keen observer. Notice immediately if you are losing energy and do something about it. Notice if your stomach begins to feel queasy or if you feel a sudden shift into anxiety. Breathe fully and observe what is happening and who is around you. Tune in to you and remind yourself of your choices, available options, and boundaries.

Do you need more space, or perhaps self-respect or self-care? What messages are you telling yourself? Are they messages from the past or from someone else? Whose voice is it? Thoughts are not you. They are thoughts. Practice mindfulness regularly, in your daily routines and not only in yoga practice. **Often ask yourself how you can stay open, relaxed, and trusting of the universe without picking up anything from anyone.**

"When we truly recognize that our beliefs are that powerful - we hold the key to freedom."

—Bruce H. Lipton, Scientist and Author of The Biology of Belief

Exercise 2 - Noticing and Blocking Energy

First, tune in to how you are feeling. How do the subtle energies feel around your solar plexus? Just notice. Can you give a few examples? Place your hands over your solar plexus as if resting them there or holding a book over the area with the intention of blocking all energies not of your highest good. How you feel? Do you notice a change from how you were feeling? Remove your hands, again tuning in to the energies around you. Once again place your hands in front of your solar plexus with the blocking intention in place. In the beginning we are simply learning to notice that there are in fact differences in the energy and information we are picking up. Over time, we will learn how to balance this flow of information.

Exercise 3: Diverting Energy

Face a partner. Ask the partner to intend to send you angry energy. For a moment intend to see, hear, know, or feel her emotional energy. Next, intend to or physically step back away from the emotional energy, then turn sideways and let the energy flow by you.

"Your destiny is bound with the destinies of others. You must either learn to carry the Universe or be crushed by it. You must grow strong enough to love the world, yet empty enough to sit down at the same table with its worst horrors."

—Andrew Boyd

7

Protections and Energetic Management

Cultivating regular practices of Energetic Management along with your normal everyday routine reaps huge dividends for empaths. Energetic Management protects and encourages health right along with brushing your teeth, bathing, and the myriad of other ways we take care of ourselves daily. These practices are part of a healthy empathic life and will raise your vibration. Try adding them to your day gradually over time and see how quickly you feel balanced, energized, and renewed.

Morning

- Begin the day with gratitude, setting intentions, yoga, meditation or something that grounds and enlivens you.

- Learn about and practice self-nurturing.

- Make a mental note and set intention of "I will not take on the emotions or energies of others."

Throughout the day

- If you are feeling overwhelmed or believe you may be picking up on energy you do not need, intend to release it when you wash your hands.

- Stay grounded and enjoy life in simple ways.

- Connect with touch stones as needed. Carry a smooth stone or shell in your pocket.

- Use resetting tools if needed. See the section Raising your Vibration, the Art of Decompression.

Evening

- Before entering your home at the end of the day, pull off all energies that do not belong to you. Gently pulling energy out through the hair is an incredible way to release negative energy. (See Energetic Taffy Pull tool in the Energetic Management section of this book.)

- Intend that any energy that was pulled from you or that you left somewhere that day be restored back to you. Is there any energy that lingers with someone you talked to that day?

- Stand up, close your eyes, and intend it home like a vacuum that only sucks up what is yours and of your highest good. Then send any aches, pains, negative thoughts, patterns or emotions, anything not of your highest good to the earth to be recycled. Imagine and feel these energies flowing down out of your fingertips into the earth. Engage in self-nurturing such as taking an Epsom salt bath or enjoying relaxing activities.

Increase your vibration, have more vitality, more energy:

Shift your consciousness towards freedom. Free yourself from the negative tyranny of energy-depleting thoughts and actions. It may take some practice, but soon you will let go of the patterns of "I should or I am sorry," being inauthentic (trying to be the person someone else wants you to be), and feeling you need to fix situations for others. Stop allowing others to tell you what you should do, whom you should be, and how you should feel. Instead, feel what you feel. You do not have to do anything. Stop worrying about what others think of you. Stop saying you are sorry. Everytime you apologize, you are discounting yourself. Over time this "unconsciously self-diminishing" platitude will deplete you and make you physically sick. If you did not step on someone's foot, why are you apologizing? If you were not causal, you are not responsible. Imagine that! One way to rid yourself of unduly saying "sorry" is to substitute the word "thank you" instead. Try saying, "Thank-you for waiting for me" instead of "I'm sorry I'm late."

Honor You! Feel your feelings fully. They are your feelings and feelings are okay. Feelings tell you something. It can be they are telling you that you are taking on something that you do not authentically want. It may be that they are telling you that you are experiencing sadness. Instead of ignoring and repressing your feelings, acknowledge and welcome them. Feelings are the marrow of life, the hallmark of existing as a whole human being on this earth. When feelings arise, ask some questions: What is behind this feeling?

What is this feeling trying to tell me? Be fully present with the emotion and then allow it to release like blessed ether to the heavens.

Release the urge to always please people and make peace for others. What is not yours to bear? You are never obligated to take on any energies. In fact, it is best that you do not do so. If a situation feels draining or heavy, you have a choice not to take on drama or negativity. Choose you, love you, nurture you, tune in to you! What feels good to you? Who are you? Without any judgment, what do you like and not like?

Instead of shutting down and pulling in when overwhelmed by outside emotions or information, raise your vibration. Intend your energy to grow, to become larger by tuning into more inspirational energy.

Sprinkle of Joy technique:

My dear friend Carlos developed this tool to raise a person's vibration to that of joy. He rubs his fingers back and forth on both hands as if dusting flour over another person, intending the vibration of joy. To my great surprise, when I asked him to try this technique on me, I could feel it. The vibration was palpable. I have discovered it also works with other positive emotions. Try it with joy: feel and intend joy, then sprinkle away. Try it with love or gratitude, then ask the person how they are feeling. Try it on yourself. Part of Empath Care is raising our own vibrations. This tool is a keeper!

Empaths need to carefully choose their tribe and be sure to select positive people to be around. This community should be made of people with whom they can talk freely about their gifts and possess safe, healthy boundaries.

How does one best help the empath in one's life?

- Be a good listener.
- Believe them! They often tell more truth than the majority of people. I have yet to meet an empath that has not suffered because they were not believed in their childhood.
- Do not label them as "moody" or "too emotional."
- Be kind and loving and give them eye contact along with your full attention.
- Understand that they have a difficult time doing something they do not like or that does not align with their sense of morality. They really would rather go hungry than usurp their own ethical beliefs.

8

The Empathic Child

This section, which is dedicated to children, may also be healing for the adult version of you. As you study the tools here, make notes about what might resonate for your child and also for your own inner child. If you are an empath, you are almost certain to have an empathic child.

Chances are if you are reading this, you are already aware that your child has empathic gifts. If, however, you are not empathic yourself and know nothing about the world of empathing, the child is often left on her own to cope with an overwhelming world. She may have unexplained behaviors and mood shifts that seem dramatic followed by emotional isolation. She may appear excessively shy, distant, or even shut down. Become an aware observer. If a mood comes out of nowhere, it maybe your child is actually empathic.

Empathic children will often be wise beyond their years. They pick up on far more information than most other children and are usually misunderstood by the educational system and adults around them. They can appear very moody and may seem dramatic or overly sensitive to the world. Levels of sensitivities may fluctuate. There may be times when your child registers an oversensitivity to sound and has a tough time blocking it out.

He may be more sensitive to the fabric on his skin or his temperature sensitivity may be off. This is called Sensory Integration Dysfunction, and some empaths may experience this condition at varying levels of intensity. They are hot when it is cold and cold when it is hot. What is important is acknowledging your child's feelings and helping him come back into a feeling of balance and control. It may mean giving him flexible plastic swimming ear plugs and talking to him about imagining a dial that can be rotated to turn the sound down. It may mean teaching him about layering his clothing and everyone realizing they need to work on their empath immune systems in filtering out what is not theirs.

Still not sure if your child is empathic? Ask them to identify how they think you may be feeling when you are feeling particularly sad. Put on a smile and a voice inflection of joyfulness and give no other clues outwardly of your true feelings but focus on your true feelings when you ask them. It is best not to do this exercise when you are in a crowd or they are playing on the playground or being in their own world.

Once you have identified that they are empathic, you are still responsible for helping them adjust to their community and the world. They may talk to you about things that bother them. Let them know that other people may not understand because they are not empaths and they have no reference for these experiences. Allow the child to be truly authentic as often as possible at home and in the world.

Empathic children are different in the following ways:

- The empathic child often "does not make sense."

- They may have extreme shifts in behavior, including unexplained tantrums.

- They may have imaginary friends and claim to see things that are not there, as far as you can tell.

- They may have an unexplained aversion to certain people, locations, or places.

- They may be calm and lovely at home then get to school and come experience emotional meltdowns.

- They sometimes have difficulty focusing in public places.

Supporting our empathic children:

The best thing you can do for children is to actively listen to them. Get off the computer, stop doing what you are doing, and look at them. Let them talk. Let them keep talking even if they sound dramatic or do not make sense: acknowledge them, validate them. This is by far one of the most important gifts you can give them. Empathic children need acceptance. Telling a child that they are dramatic, wrong, imagining it, or should "toughen up" is the very last thing they need. Yet, that is the most common way that our culture deals with highly sensitive people. Many children end up shutting down their gifts and becoming hardened. They learn to disconnect as a long-term coping mechanism.

- Help calm them on a cold morning by offering them warm herbal tea and beginning the day with a peaceful spirit.

- Let them play in the mud or in the sand at the beach, blow bubbles, or play for hours at a time.

- Allow them to color or paint and explore creative outlets.

- Provide a beautiful, uncluttered space for them.

- Recognize that they are more likely to enjoy playing with one friend rather than a group.

Being aware that they are empathic is the first step! Their teachers will often report that they daydream when instructions are being given, then they act out in class. They try to escape the torture of sitting still for long hours by retreating into their imaginations. Non-traditional school systems may serve your empathic child best. Waldorf or homeschool programs might prove to be your top choice. The way your child learns may look very different, as empaths often have a difficult time engaging in activities they do not enjoy. Sometimes empathic children resent being clumped into groups.

They may find it difficult to sit next to particular people who trigger their sensitivities, for example. These alternative schools tend to allow for more time in nature, more time with the spirit or soul side of the child. They often accommodate a more natural way of learning that is better suited to the empathic child. If public school is what is available to your child, then spend extra time with her in nature as often as you can. It is especially important for empathic children to feel the healing qualities of the earth on their skin. Let them get dirty! Let them experience the joy of unstructured play for hours at a time to rebalance their energies and calm their souls.

It is critical to never force your child to listen to you unload your adult issues. It is not your child's job to balance you. You can't hide your emotions from your child, but it is your responsibility to balance your life first.

Gently offer teachings of how he or she can apply the tools given in this book as him and her are ready. Realize that each empath has her own journey, despite our best efforts. Teach him and her to clear all energy in their field before going to bed. Have them tune into this calming practice before he or she goes to sleep. Help them appreciate who they are at their core along with their divine abilities. Let them know in their bones that their home is the safest place to talk about their gifts and sensitivities. Teach them about identifying and feeling their feelings and they will be healthier and happier for it.

Most empathic children feel a rawness in the world. Crowded spaces often overwhelm them. Recognizing this and empowering them with the tools in this book will help. We want them to learn who they are without the influence of others, then feel comfortable expressing who they are authentically, even while surrounded by the presence of others. Finding ways to identify and hear their internal messaging systems allows the input of others to float by them instead of through them. When they act out or become loud, try to understand that they are attempting to be louder than the emotional noise of their environment.

These children will know when you are not speaking your truth. Assure them that you are "working on it" if they inquire about what they are picking up from you. Do not worry about things in front of them if you can help it. If you lie to them, they will feel insecure about their natural gifts. Teach them about not taking on the emotions or problems of others. Teach them to say a prayer for someone they are worried about or do distance Reiki if they feel compelled to help. Then help them learn how to let go of it.

If you are not with them when the world feels overwhelming, here are a few techniques that may be helpful:

- Suggest that they tune in to the calm friend who is usually happy when they are at school. This may help them with regaining their balance a bit. Help them understand that it is a good idea to tune in to how they are feeling around various peers and–it is within their power to choose calm and happy every chance they get.

- Help them remember that the empath's natural tendency is to "help" the underdog, the ones who suffer the most in school. They may benefit from praying for the underdog friend or sending him distance Reiki rather than trying to be the only person to befriend him.

- Remind empathic children that the same holds true if they feel the need to do something for a hurt animal or sad situation. Praying or energetic self-treatment empowers them to help themselves each and every day.

- Teach them that learning to balance their personal needs with their desire to help others is the key.

- In times of emotional distress, ask them to place their hand on their heart and feel their heart beating. Ask them if they can slow their heartbeat by mindfully breathing in and out. Can they feel their heartbeat slow down just a little bit?

- Help them to visualize external feedback as energy and to "step inside their cloak of protection" to allow the external feedback to harmlessly pass by.

- Have the child look into your eyes or focus on your calming smile. Make sure looking into an adult's eyes is culturally acceptable to the child.

- Take the child to a quieter room, or if at a noisy place like a theme park, find a real tree or plant outside for him to focus on. Ask the tree to help calm him.

- Allow empathic children their fill of water play time in nature and outdoors, if this is a possibility.

- Help them acknowledge and accept their needs even if they seem different. If they are in a loud environment for example, empower them with comfortable ear plugs they can put in and adjust as needed.

Balancing activities, quiet time

Empathic children need more quiet time than other children do. They also require more time in nature to play. Playing hard in water or nature to run or swim off their excess energy is a wonderful plan unless there are too many people or something negative in the area. These children can easily become overwhelmed in large crowds and you may see behavior problems bubble up very quickly.

How can you help them?

Accept them as they are, allow them to make shifts for their own comfort levels. Do not over-schedule their time. They need more time to decompress than other children. Avoid places and activities that over stimulate them to help them transition into a relaxed state after a long day.

Encourage them to take a bath or shower to wash the energy of school away before settling into homework. If they cannot take a bath, perhaps changing into clean comfy clothes and making use of some essential oils are another recommendation. Such centering activities may also help calm the child if he becomes overwhelmed or overly stressed.

Do not discount the feelings of an empathic child. When you do this, you are telling him that you do not believe him. Over time this can shut him down and leave him feeling isolated and alone.

If an empathic child says he or she does not like how a room feels, you may want to do address this in whichever way is most relevant as they are often correct in their perceptions. If he or she does not like playing at certain people's houses, do not ignore this. Choose your child's tribe carefully.

The emotions of those around him and her can influence them profoundly. Empathic children are known for taking on the preferences and behaviors of the people with whom they spend time. Teach them to notice if they only act a certain way when they are with that particular person. Ask them to start identifying what is their own and what is someone else's.

An empathic child will have an acute intuition about people. Teach them to trust his intuition. If they feel someone is not right for them to be around, believe them. They are right. Do not make a big deal about it. Just acknowledge them and do not make plans with that person anymore.

When empaths ignore their intuition and feel they have no sense of control over their sensitivities or that they are imagining a false reality, they often step into self-abuse, negative self-talk loops, limited beliefs, and anxiety patterns. If any of this resonates with your childhood past, feel free to consider ways to begin healing your past and learn to tune in to your belly wisdom (gut feeling) again.

Empathic children's emotions

Empathic children have hyper sensitivities, often an overload of incoming information from their senses. They often have some sensory integration imbalances such as feeling the seams in socks or tags from clothing more than other people. They can hear more, see more, smell more and know more than most. If you are not an empath, just imagine what that would be like.

Emotions are not always felt as the child's own. They can also know the underlying emotions of another and this knowing may cause problems like not trusting their own intuition, not trusting others and more. The emotions of others are often picked up in a negative way by the child.

For example, if the teacher is angry, even if she smiles and does not say she is angry, the empathic child may think she is angry at them and believe they have done something wrong, or that they are not good enough in some way. Teach them about their gifts and their challenges.

Make them aware that what they may be feeling at any given moment may not be something we can see or that is obvious to others. Teach them that they have a soul, a spirit side. They can feel other energies as though they are coming from within themselves.

Teach them that the feelings of others are not their concern most of the time and that they should not spend any time trying to detect them. General compassion for others is a good thing and something we need more of in this world, however, empathic children are prone to over identifying with the sufferings of others. They lack no capacity for compassion, rather, their challenge is to seek a healthy balance that is sustainable for them.

Talk to them about creating protective bubbles, engaging in prayer practices, setting intentions, cultivating healthy emotions and sensing and setting boundaries. Intend to let in only love and things that are good for them and to block out anything not helpful.

I often talk to adults about the normal processes of emotions. I tell them that if they feel like crying, it is a beautiful thing to allow themselves that release. When we are born, we cry to release feelings, to let others know how we are feeling, to alert others we have a need. It is our natural release system for sadness and other emotions. It seems our culture has done much to shut down this natural release system, especially for boys and men, as crying is sometimes seen as a weakness.

When instructing preschool teachers, I often ask them to recall times when children have been hurt during playtime. Did each child get to cry and voice their feelings about what happened? Did a well-meaning teacher brush him off and tell him that he was fine, thereby preventing him from crying and discounting his feelings? Take for instance a common occurance on a preschool playground.

Two three year old boys, Johnny and Gabe play together outside on the playground. Johnny pushes Gabe forcefully and Gabe falls to the ground and hits his head. If a teacher can listen to Gabe's hurt feelings and let him cry, Gabe will be able to process his emotions. If the teacher can invite Johnny to recognize Gabe's pain and express how he thinks Gabe feels, Johnny's emotional intelligence and compassion for others grows. Gabe now feels acknowledged. It is helpful to foster communication between the two children. If we allow time for this process, the next day Gabe and Johnny play together again and all will be well. If we do not acknowledge the conflict and emotional turmoil and allow the body to process emotions in a natural releasing way, in 40 years Gabe may still retain negative trapped emotions and beliefs that deeply affect him and the way he responds to others in the world.

Empathic children and medical care

Some empathic children pick up and transmute the aches, pains and ailments of others. Let's say the child suddenly complains of knee pain and no recent accident or injury event has occurred. Ask yourself if the child has been around someone with knee pain today. Ask the child if she noticed knee pain in someone else today. Sometimes the child will know exactly who had knee pain.

Have them ask themselves if the pain is truly their pain. Do they sense that it may belong to someone else? The priority is to build the child's empathic immunity. When it comes to physical ailments, the key is to listen, acknowledge, evaluate, and self-treat with the intention to release and re-evaluate.

Sometimes when children feel pain, they are not necessarily sick or injured in such a situation. It becomes a priority to step away from the illness paradigm. Help them set an intention about what they will pick up and what is not allowed in. Teach them about staying connected to the energy of their physical body at all times, to "be in the body," and help them learn to clear what is not needed. Teach the child to physically grab the energy of the knee pain and have them pull it off with their hands and send it to the earth. If the child notices a dramatic shift, repeat the pulling-off exercise. Then help them learn how to listen to the place that is hurting, ask the area what it is saying, empathize and acknowledge the pain, and send the knee the intention of healing love. If, the knee still hurts then you may want to ensure there is nothing seriously wrong with the knee. This practice, of course, can be used for any number of empathic energies in practically any part of the body.

Empathic children often experience stomach aches. This may occur because they feel responsible for fixing others. Sometimes they carry the burden of the adults around them, such as inappropriate worry (for their age), i.e. feeling concerned about their parents financial problems.

If empaths do not care for themselves in a healthy way, through self care, healthy boundaries and relationships, an overall balanced lifestyle - they are likely to get sick in some way over time. They must learn energy management, to clearly set their intentions, protect themselves, eat real and healthy food, and find ways of refilling and balancing.

Empathic children are particularly soulful. They experience other dimensions, of which many are not aware, and and about which we are not taught in modern society. It is important to teach these children how to pray. They do not need to adhere to a particular religion or dogma while praying, but may focus on what is most comfortable to the child, be it the divine, angelic help, or nature's energy. For example, if they see a dead animal and it is upsetting their day, they may feel some control by helping to pray for the animal. This activity will help the child to let go of the distress, as well as help the animal as it transitions.

If the upset lingers, teach them to blow their breath out of their hands, whooshing their intentions away, sending their prayers to the animal's soul so the anguish does not remain with the child. They can also rub their hands back and forth as they are wiping their hands. Please see next picture.

In a similar vein, it is very important to listen to our empathic children, acknowledge what they experience, then give them tools for self-evaluation and self-help. Ask them to consider time spent with a friend, and if feelings they experienced with this friend were their own. Did anyone else feel those sensations around them at the same time? Or ask, "How do you feel after spending time with Bobby today? Did you talk about Bobby's interests, or things you both like?" Asking these simple questions, allows the subconscious mind to consider that certain feelings, may in fact, not belong to the child, but, rather her friend.

Therefore, when they become conscious of the possible melding of emotions, with another's emotions, a level of healing occurs. Initially, they may resist talking about their feelings and experiences as an empath, but over time you can assist them in learning more about them. Gradually they can begin the process of identifying what is theirs and what belongs to someone else. Also, they will learn what they enjoy and do not enjoy with or without the influence of others. This is vital for each child to know.

"Empathetic listening is an awesome medication for the hurting heart."

Gary Chapman, Author
of *The Five Love Languages*

Exercise 4: Releasing Someone Else's Emotion(s)

Imagine the other person's emotion leaving like dust floating out of them and falling onto the ground. Imagine or intend pulling that emotion off of them—knowingly grabbing the emotion and throwing it to the ground for recycling.

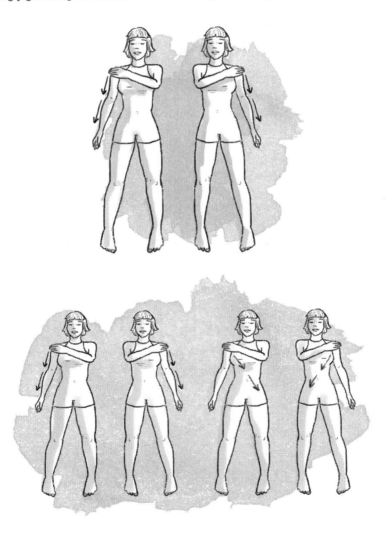

Exercise 5: Releasing My Own Emotion(s)

We also want to want to help our young empaths understand that they may be deeply compassionate while simultaneously refusing to absorb anything from others. Ask the child to identify which feelings they are experiencing.

Tell them to pick the strongest one, then really, really feel it. If it is anger, instruct them to clench their hands, allow anger to rise for a few seconds, then if they are ready to release it they may visualize dropping it on the ground or letting if float out of them

If he or she is not ready to let it go, encourage them to continue feeling this anger as intensely as they can. Then ask them to tell you when the are ready or want to let it go. Repeat if they notice other emotions—or in the case of ailments, more feeling states in the body, mind, or soul. This exercise will help them to release negative emotions within themselves rather than repressing them.

Home and Environments

Transition and detox at the end of each day:

It is important to clear ourselves from the influences of our day before coming into the house by simply asking our guides to completely clear any and all negative energies for our highest good. Consider the crossover clearing practice mentioned earlier: cross the body, and clear down the arms a few times. To cleanse or detox yourself and your environment in other ways, you may:

- Bathe, shower, or change clothes

- Keep the environment chemical free. Do not use chemical-laden products, like conventional cleaning agents; cigarettes; perfume, cologne, air fresheners, or any other kind of synthetic scents; etc.

- Make sure the empathic child's environment is safe, uncluttered, and comfortable. Keep the home calm

- Avoid violence of any kind, be it on television or in person (such as arguing)

- Seriously limit screen time (for yourself and your children) as many empaths are highly sensitive to EMFs—environment energies from electronics

- Be very selective about what your empathic children view

As an instructor in child development courses at the college level, I often send students home with instructions to watch 3 television shows designed for children and count the number of negative things said or done. Students are often surprised at the frequency with which violent acts and hurtful comments occur in a typical Saturday morning cartoon. It is the responsibility of the parents, especially those children who are empathic, to only watch television after the child has gone to bed, if these shows are violent, consider using earbuds or perhaps turning the television sound down very low. Empathic children who hear someone scream, even in their sleep, often have terrible nightmares. Children may not seem like they are paying attention, but they are easily imprinted upon by experiences and upset by what is reflected on the screen. They connect too deeply with the images and the people or animals affected. These resonances stay with them and may cause anxiety.

Monster Spray:

Materials:

Spray bottle, I recommend a 6-ounce size for easy handling

Water (fill the bottle three-quarters full)

1 Tablespoon Witch hazel

Essential oils:

10 drops Lavender essential oil

5 drops Clary sage essential oil

5 drops *Grounding Essential Oil blend

If desired, use a permanent marker to label the spray bottle and draw symbols that help the child feel good, such as a sun or some Reiki healing symbols.

Directions:

Shake the spray bottle to mix ingredients. Spray around the child's bed, under the bed or in the closets. Let the child spray or direct this activity. Monster spray really works! Give it a try the next time the child feels overly anxious.

Essential oils calm the child and help foster healthy sleep practices. Specific oils are fantastic for clearing the space—note how much better it feels to enter a room after they are sprayed. They are safe and effective in assisting the child to shift into a deep restorative sleep; just be sure to use them as directed. It is our job to help our empathic children feel safe as we validate their emotional needs and empower them to cleanse and reclaim their space. When they express their fears or tell you what they are seeing, show confidence that the monster spray will absolutely help and allow them to spray ahead of time if need be. Lavender oil has a natural calming and soothing effect and is often used for insomnia. Witch hazel has a preservative effect and helps disperse oils evenly throughout water. Clary sage is a clearing, protective oil that promotes restful sleep. The *"Balance Blend" promotes tranquility and calmness. You may also sage the house regularly to clear the energies in the house.

*to find out more, you are welcome to visit aprilwalker.com/essentialoils

9

Building Empathic Immunity

(Learning What Is Yours and What Is Not)

Empaths may be susceptible to anxiety, depression and illness because they absorb the experiential energies of others if not practicing the art of empathic immunity. Begin the journey of learning what is yours and what is not.

Exercise 6: Mine or Yours?

Simply ask, "Is this mine?" This subtle yet powerful question helps even if you don't feel a complete command of all the empathic immunity tools just yet. Merely by asking, "Is this mine?" you have created a mindful pause, a space for your subconscious to detach from energy if it is not yours. Just by asking the question, you have created a sacred space for yourself energetically.

- You may choose not to empath! You can direct your subconscious to begin the process of not empathing what is not good for you. You have free will. You get to make decisions about empathing or not empathing. Just because you can do it does not mean you should or that you must empath.

- If you still struggle after learning all that is offered in this book, find a **Body Code** practitioner to assist you in identifying and clearing the underlying issues that persist. There are times when doing this yourself does not serve you.

- Remember that continually saving people does not serve you or them. It may in fact create codependency and a karmic energetic debt.

Write your feelings and observations:

10

What to Do When...

... you feel drained, anxious, overwhelmed, and you find yourself taking on extra physical weight to protect yourself from observing emotional and energetic negativity.

Exercise 7: "Bubble Shield"

Stand facing a partner. Let's call her Linda. Ask her to remember something sad or anger- provoking and to feel that emotion. Can you pinpoint the moment she connected to that emotion? Yes, now practice giving it back to her. Once you sense the emotion, you are done. You've identified it! Now can you work on not picking up or owning Linda's emotion? Doing so does not mean you are unable or unwilling to experience empathy—it simply means that you do not bring her emotion into your energy field. Practice discerning between feeling and knowing. Notice how that feeling is hers, not yours. Then it will be your turn to feel your emotion and your partner's turn to practice building their empathic immunity. Once you feel more comfortable sensing another's emotion, you can practice directing this emotion back toward her using the same steps outlined above. Simply send her emotion toward her after you notice she has connected to it. She can practice blocking your intention, and you can switch to strengthen your empathic immunity.

Learn about the valuable action of shielding your energetic field. Imagining and intending, surrounding yourself with a flexible bubble of light. Remember, an empath's intentions are very powerful. Let your imagination choose a color, if you find it helpful. Intend that your shield will turn negative energies into positive energies to help protect you from electromagnetic toxins as well. The bubble is flexible. It allows in all love and good things as it filters out all energies that do not serve you as well.

- Practice shielding with a partner
- Practice feeling energetic shifts
- Turn your back and practice again

Write your feelings and observations:

Exercise 8: Lean in/Lean out — the Donkey Exercise

My late grandmother visited the holy city of Jerusalem in her eighties. She traveled with a group and rode a donkey up a steep mountain. She expressed her trepidation about the narrowness of the path, fearing that she would tumble over the edge of the cliff with her donkey, or that her knee would be crushed against the narrow precipice. The donkeys walked two by two up the hill with their trusting passengers. When the path narrowed, they would lean into each other for protection. The moment the path widened again, they would separate.

Practice awareness of blending, entangling, and separating on purpose. Trust your inner donkey but keep an eye on your own path. Lean in to discern the emotions—but when the time comes, take your separate path and stay protected.

Exercise: Find a partner and grasp one end of a yoga belt or long cord, giving the other end to your partner. Face one another with a few feet of space between you and practice holding with just enough pressure to keep the belt tight. Too much pulling of the belt means that one person is tugged forward. Too little pressure and the belt will fall slack. Practice staying even and balanced with the energy needed for the belt to maintain an even keel, sensing your partner's field and your own.

What sensations did you experience while balancing your donkey on the path? Did you feel like rescuing your partner? Could you tell when to lean in and help, when to accept help yourself, and when to return to your own path?

11

Protect and Raise Your Vibration: The Art of Decompression

Empaths survive and thrive when they prioritize self-care in their lives. An empath can relax and raise his or her vibration in various ways. In this section, I offer a variety of positive self-practice modalities. I encourage daily practice of one or more of these activities. Feel free to explore many different techniques to find out what works best for you.. It's wise to practice regularly, cycling through the different healing practices. What brings you bliss, nourishes your soul, magnifies your feel good vibes? What brings you down? We want more of the good, less of the negative.

- Solar Plexus Balance: Bring your hands to your solar plexus area, intend loving healing there, breathe light to refill self-love, and ask for divine love and light to fill you.

- When someone is particularly draining, **cover the back of the neck** and intend your energy to be retained and not be released.

- Spend time in nature, every chance you get. Empaths refill and regenerate by connecting to nature. The ocean and the mountains are particularly beneficial.

- Connect with the energy of a tree. Literally hug a tree, or sit with your back to it and ask the tree to help you reconnect with the energy of the earth to heal you.

- Connect with the ocean from a beach. Negative ions are abound at the ocean and numerous studies suggest that these molecules impart impressive health benefits, from stress reduction to mood stabilization. A meta-analysis assessing over thirty studies concluded that exposure to negative ions correlated substantively with reduced depression, especially as the density of negative ions increased. Inhale the negative ions and ask the ocean to send relaxing, revitalizing energy to you as it takes away your stress.

A vital exercise for building your empathic immunity is to spend a few minutes connecting with nature. The ocean is one of the most healing places on the planet with its abundance of healing negative ions. Intend and be willing to feel and know the energy of the ocean. Now meld the energy from your environment and your own energy. Feel and know the energy of yourself. Notice the difference between the two. Practicing this alone in nature builds the empathic immune system in powerful ways, which will later assist you in more hectic public environments. This skill helps you make the healthy choice to stay in your own energy field and tune out unhealthy input from electrical signals and other people.

- Also, invest in a **salt lamp**, the negative ions are helpful in reducing stress and releasing emotions.

- Practice **earthing**, connecting to the earth's natural energy by making direct contact between your feet and other parts of your body to the revitalizing energy of the earth.

- If you visit a public place like a shopping mall, take a positive energy friend and allow them to act as a buffer.

Visualization, meditation and intention – the studies on the powers of these tools are conclusive. When we calm the body and mind, clarity of where energy begins and ends is greatly enhanced:

- **Meditation and intention** enhances the mind/body connection and edifies our awareness of the intricately integrated system of our being. For example, imagine you have a beautiful yellow Meyer lemon in your hands. Smell the lemon, feel the delicately dimpled texture of the soft outer skin, soak in the bright yellow essence and rousing scent. Next, envision slicing the lemon on a cutting board. See the juice burst out as you slice. Bring the juicy sour lemon to your mouth and take a bite. Now notice that even though you have not actually taken a bite, the moisture in your mouth has increased. The body has responded to the visualization.

  Close your eyes and imagine you're able to control volume or the amount of information you are receiving. This simple visualization moves the unconscious mind to regulate input in a healthy way.

- **Meditation** calms the mind and connects the physical and energetic bodies. Even a few minutes of practice brings forth clearer thinking throughout the day. There are many ways of practicing meditation and all empaths benefit from practicing some form of meditation. However, for empaths, it is most important to set an intention of connecting to their authentic self.

- **Practice daily gratitude and positive affirmations**: these practices keep you in the positive realm and raise your vibration. Every day spend 3 to 5 minutes writing 1 to 3 things you are grateful for. Sometimes words are insufficient to contain our gratitude, so try a photo instead. There are several phone apps that make gratitude journals easy and fun. Later you can sift through your positive memories and remember how good life is.

- **Labyrinths** – walking meditations with ancient reverberations.

- **Time in water** – empaths feel better around water

- **Soak** in a bath at home with epsom salt, baking soda, lavender essential oil, or find a sensory deprivation float tank at a favorite salon or spa and relax.

- Spend time in or near rivers, lakes, creeks, salt water swimming pools. **Water aerobics** is a phenomenal way to reduce stress.

- A warm relaxing **shower** can change your mood, cleanse the physical body and the auric field.

- Practice moving energy with **Yoga**. Yoga is about more than fitness. Yoga supports a healthy and happy mind/body/spirit connection. Yoga assists the empath with being in body and moving through stuck energies.

- Engage in regular **exercise** for endorphins and detoxing.

Breathing techniques are amazing for decompression. They can reduce anxiety and overwhelm fast, relax the nervous system and help a person to feel more grounded in just a few minutes. See detailed information on various Breathing Techniques in Chapter 16.

Exercise 9: Child's Pose

This pose helps you get back in touch with your own energy. It assists in disconnecting you from the outer world a bit and helps you release, ground, and center. Take one to three deep breaths in this pose. Begin on your hands and knees. Spread your knees wide apart while keeping your big toes touching. Rest your buttocks on your heels. Those with very tight hips can keep their knees and thighs together. Sit up straight and lengthen your spine. On an exhalation, bow forward, bringing your torso between your thighs. Your heart and chest should rest between or on top of your thighs. Allow your forehead to come to the floor. Keep your arms long and extended, palms facing down. Press back slightly with your hands to keep your buttocks in contact with your heels. Lengthen from your hips to your armpits, and then extend even further through your fingertips. Let your upper back broaden.

Soften and relax your lower back. Allow all tension in your shoulders, arms, and neck to drain away. Hold for up to a minute or longer, breathing softly. To release the pose, gently use your hands to walk your torso upright to sit back on your heels.

Cautions:

Do not practice Child's Pose if you have a current or recent knee injury. Women who are pregnant should only practice a wide-legged variation of the pose. Always work within your own range of limits and abilities. Try child's pose for a few minutes or as it feels good, then write about how you feel and what you notice:

12

Meditation and Mudras

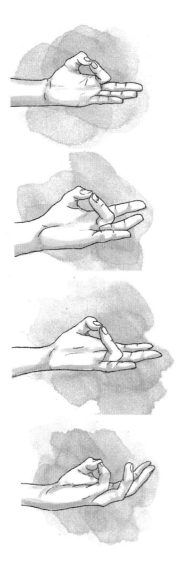

Guyan Mudra: Thumb touches tip of index finger, other fingers extended. This position brings more energy to the lower body, encouraging deeper states of calmness.

Shuni Mudra: Thumb touches tip of middle finger, other fingers extended. This position cultivates patience and encourages good energetic metabolism. It helps empaths avoid adding body weight as a means of protection, encouraging them to stay safely inside their own awareness.

Surya Ravi Mudra: Thumb touches tip of ring finger. This position assists us with energy stability.

Buddi Mudra: Thumb touches tip of pinky finger, other fingers extended. This position resolves connections to the feeling body and encourages awareness towards more authentic communication.

Apan Mudra: Middle and ring finger fold in and touch thumb. This position assists in detoxifying our bodies from everything that is not ours.

Ruhdra Mudra: The middle and ring fingertips touch the thumb. This position relieves stress and anxiety.

Vayu Mudra: The index finger tip touches the thumb. This position assist regulation of mental and physical connections.

13

Essential Oils for Empaths

Essential oils, particularly those grown in their natural habitat, can raise a person's vibration. By being absorbed by the skin and inhaled, they affect the limbic system, which is the part of the brain that affects emotions. If you are having a difficult time in crowds or work and you cannot leave, place a drop of a calming essential oil such as lavender or balance blend on the 3rd eye to assist in balancing and boundary incoming energies. This truly helps; try it. Be careful not to let the lavender essential oil come in contact with your eyes as it is a very strong healing agent and may burn the sensitive tissues of the eyes.

Properties of Essential Oils:

Shielding and protecting:

Clary sage helps uplift, soothe and balance heightened emotions and clear negative enegeries. Clary Sage is a beautiful oil to diffuse for a calming aroma when you feel worry or anxiousness. It can also be used to promote relaxation in preparation for a restful night's sleep.

Geranium is used for protection worldwide, it keeps negative energies at bay. One drop of Geranium's sweet aroma per day in an armpit for additional level of sacred peace. It can support clearing the energies of others and otherness for empaths who are sensitive to those who have passed. The aroma of Geranium oil can also help lessen feelings of stress and calm nerves.

Grounding:

Clary-sage is a powerful clearing, grounding, protective oil, good for insomnia, anxiety, negative emotions and energies.

Rosemary helps to ground and increase focus. Peppermint is energizing, exhilarating and helps to raise vibration.

Grounding Blend* effective grounding, calms anxiety, provides clarity and emotional healing.

Refilling, relaxing

Lavender promotes instant relaxation for mind, body and soul. Clears negative emotions, also for protection from negative emotions and chemicals such as perfumed products. Helps you relax and sleep. Lemon grass - to do past life and karmic healing.

Lemon clears the emotions of others out of your field.

Basil calms anxiety, lifts fatigue and depression.

Frankincense ultimate grounding and healing. Assists in helping Empath to recognize the difference between their own emotions and the emotions of others.

*To find out more, you are welcome to visit aprilwalker.com/essentialoils

14

Smudging Tools for Empaths

Smudging is a simple cleansing activity that has been believed to be used by Native Americans for centuries. A daily act of cleansing and purification acts as an aromatic smoke bath for the human energy field. The smoke is believed to release negative vibrations, bringing on a more positive mood. There are also benefits such as clearing the air of mold spores, pollen, pet dander and more. Smudging yourself and your home helps to reduce stress, improve sleep and clear the air. You can even clear objects of negative vibrations with smudging. Typically, the smudge aromatic is burned over an ocean shell or piece of pottery. One basic way to smudge is to first, intend to clear negative energy. Perhaps begin with a prayer to release anything that is no longer serving you. Thank the herbs. Put herbs into a shell or other fireproof dish and light them. Blow out the flame allowing the herbs to to smoke Using a feather or your hand start above you head fluffing the smoke toward you working your way down the body in this way. Notice the shifts you feel energetically. There are many options for aromatic smudging, here are a few of my favorites:

- White Sage - to release the troubled mind, clear bacteria energies, infection energies.

- Cedar - to release anger and intensity energies

- Palo Santo - Holy Wood to release negative energies, illness, anxiety energy

- Bay leaf - to lift depression energies

15

Healing with Sound, Crystals, and Stones

Tuning forks – tuning forks are easily used to clear the field of negative emotions. **Singing bowls** – to clear negativity and balance the mind and body. **Music** can change a mood in a couple of minutes. Headsets and music may also be used to block out the world and assist with inner focus. **Exercise** in building empath immunity: To understand more about how sound and music can affect you, play 3 minutes of a negative screaming music selection – stop and notice how you feel afterwards. Then, play 3 minutes of classical music – stop and notice the difference of how you feel now.

Crystals and stones for Empaths:

Empaths have unique needs in protections, grounding and clarity. Crystals and stones can provide energetic shifts and are often appealing to look at. Crystals and stones do need to be cleared now and again.

How to clear crystals? Here are several options:

- They may be cleared by asking your spirit guides to clear them completely for highest good daily.
- Reiki power symbol over the top with intention to clear them.
- Place under the moon overnight.
- Place in salt for 24 hours.

Here are some examples of stones that are helpful for empaths:

- **Amethyst**: Calming stone, psychic protection.
- **Black Tourmaline**: Said to be a guardian mineral stone for empaths. This stone assists in keeping psychic energies at bay.
- **Citrine**: Balances the gut (gut feelings) and regenerates your own energy field as well as shields your aura and keeps negative energies away.
- **Chrysanthemum stone**: Assists with personal boundaries and wards off negative energies.
- **Hematite**: Soothes emotions, protective, assists in fending off negative energies.
- **Labradorite**: Keeps empaths from absorbing the energies around them by providing a protective shield. Anti-anxiety, anti-stress stone. Clears the meridians of blocked energies and unhealthy emotions.
- **Lepidolite**: Helps an empath tune out feelings that they do not need and assists the physical body to become less fatigued. Eases anxiety.
- **Rose quartz**: Helps an empath soothe and heal their own emotions. Unconditional love.
- **Malachite**: Helps remove stagnant emotional energy and assists better sleep.
- **Pyrite**: Assists with refilling depleted energy.
- **Sugilite**: Protects from energy vampires, entity attacks and other negative lower thought forms.
- **Turquoise** – breaks up negative energy and helps an empath stay in body, grounded. Recommended for sensitive children.
- **Other: Nature's gifts: shells, polished glass, rocks**. These items all carry grounding vibrations from the earth.

Exercise 10: Connecting with Nature

Hold your non-dominant hand palm down over various stones. Do you notice an energy shift over any of them? What feelings do you notice as you hold various stones? Do the stones feel different from one another energetically? Try carrying one of the stones listed above around in your pocket for a day. Did you observe any differences in your day? Make notes of what you notice. Try a different stone another day. If other people have an effect on you that makes you feel "off" in some way – put distance between you and them. Stones may be used for overcoming feeling overwhelmed in crowded places. It assists in blocking out incoming energies and assists in centering and calming. Notes:

16
Other Tools That Help Empaths

- **Take a Reiki class** – learn on a deeper level about self-treating, protecting and cultivating a tool box of methods for helping others without draining your energy. Undergoing Reiki attunements offers incredible personal healing opportunities, including clearing and realigning all energy chakras in the body, increasing the ability to connect with and **replenish life force energy**.

- Take a **muscle testing class** to give you a way of asking questions and receiving information without "feeling and sensing everything".

- **Bio Mat** for balancing the muscles, negative ion treatment and amethyst crystal treatment.

- **Perform Nurturing self-practices regularly**.

- Peaceful, simple, beautiful and uncluttered environments feed your energy and cleanses what does not serve you. Clutter deeply interferes with an empath's thinking and adds to the feeling of being overwhelmed.

- If feeling overwhelmed or angry, clean your house and you will feel a lot better. As simple as that sounds, it's true.

- High vibration live foods such as cultured foods (kefir, sauerkraut, and kombucha) add important minerals, vitamins and energy. Learn more about these foods and how to introduce them in your diet.

- Eat as many vegetables and as few chemicals as possible.

- Water intake recommendations for energetic-sensitives is half their body weight in ounces per day starting with 1 – 2 cups first thing in the morning and about a cup an hour throughout the day. Intend to bless and clear your water.

- Intend to bless and clear your food when you eat and be grateful for it.

- Practice placing the word "gratitude" on your water bottle, then pay attention to see if you feel and or notice the difference in how you feel.

- Create a sacred space at home, in a garden or uncluttered peaceful place with only the things that help you feel calm. Spend time there each day.

- Avoid negative people, places, media and entertainment.

- Choose enjoyable positive everything.

17
Breathing Techniques

As empaths, we often unconsciously hold our breath while holding on to the emotions of others. It is helpful for some empaths to place more focus on the exhale. Keeping your breathing as smooth as silk with an equal inhale and exhale helps us to check in with our emotions and support a well-grounded, balanced and healthy state of mind. A natural belly breathing state encourages us to not pick up energy that is not our own. Observe a baby or a puppy lying on his back breathing naturally. You will see his chest and the belly rising and falling. As adult empaths, we don't usually follow this natural relaxing flow. We must be mindful and practice self-healing activities that re-connect us to our physical bodies. It is important for an empath to learn and practice breathing exercises, they can be practiced any time of the day or night. They do, however, require some awareness and practice. Combine breathing techniques and visualizations to assist you in clearing and calming overwhelming emotions.

Exercise 11: First Love Breathing

Our breath is our first love. It is our first act of consciousness at birth, inhaling the miracle of life. From that moment, our autonomous nervous system takes over. Breathing becomes an unconscious, disconnected affair almost separate from us. But concentrating on breath, our first love, brings divine healing. Healthy breath flow is fundamental to increasing wellness through our life force. Breathing correctly equals increased life force and wellness. This is a vital step for empaths.

Reconnect to your natural breathing state. Lying on your back or sitting in a relaxed position, place one of your hands on your belly, just below your navel. As you inhale allow your breath to expand the lungs and thereby move the diaphragm. Feel the belly move out as if filling a balloon with air. Then on the exhale, feel the belly contract back into place. All too often we are only engaging in shallow chest breathing and that is our stressed-state breathing, not a natural balanced and healthy breathing pattern. It takes practice over time to notice when we are shallow breathing and to make corrections. But you will notice a significant shift in having more energy once you practice it over time and it becomes more natural.

After practicing this breathing a few times, add your mindfulness practices of intention. Breathe in life force, vitality and good vibrations; breathe out stress, tension and discomfort. Repeat this breath and intention practice 3 to 5 cycles and notice how you feel.

Exercise 12: Pause Breath

For fast stress reduction, relaxation and grounding. It also helps empaths remember how large their lungs truly are and helps them to stay connected to the body. Too often our energy leaves the body, leaving a feeling of disconnection rather than communion. Practice exhaling with the intention of clearing and not taking on negative energies. This is taught in many energy therapy traditions as a protection from picking up energy that is not yours.

- Breath in as much air as is possible. Fully and deeply expand the lungs, then pause, holding the breath for a count of 1, 2, 3, then exhale fully to the extent that you think you cannot possibly exhale any more, and pause at the bottom for 1...2...3... long seconds.

- Repeat this exercise for three rounds.

- Then stop and breath normally. Close your eyes for a moment and notice how you feel.

Exercise 13: Nadi Shodhana

Nadi Shodhana "alternate nostril breathing" is a well-known yoga breathing technique: To quickly shift out of overwhelming anxiety, harmonize the left and right hemispheres of the brain (which correlate to the logical and emotional sides of our personality), aid in purifying and balancing the nadis (subtle energy channels), and support a smooth flow of prana (life force) in the body. Nadi Shodhana invites a dramatic calming effect over the nervous system and also aids in maintaining body temperature.

- **Sit comfortably with a tall spine**. Let go of any tension from your jaw, shoulders, or hips. Close your eyes.

- **Relax the soft palate in the top back of your mouth**. If it helps, gently rest the tip of your tongue behind your front teeth, gently, relaxed. That's the important message. Savor the moist coolness of your breath as it slips over your soft palate for a few moments here in pure awareness.

- Place your left hand on your left knee with the palm facing upward, or in a Mudra (see Mudras above) by gently pressing the index and thumb together.

- Place the tip of the index finger and middle finger of the right hand between the eyebrows with the ring finger and little finger on the left nostril, and the thumb on the right nostril. Use the ring finger and little finger to gently depress the crease of the left nostril which will render it closed, forcing you to breathe through the right, and alternately use the thumb to gently press the right nostril closed, breathing through the left.

- One additional tip: The nostrils are comprised of erectile tissue, like a few other parts of the human body. If you just press the entire nostril to close it, it's possible to experience a slight swelling in nostril tissue, which can leave a slight stuffiness feeling afterwards. To avoid this, gently depress starting at the top of the Supra Alar Crease of your nostril to close it, rather than just applying pressure to the entire nostril.

- On an exhale, close the right nostril with your thumb and breathe out through the left nostril.

- Breathe in through the left nostril and then close with the ring finger.

- Release the thumb on the right nostril and breathe out through the right nostril.

- Inhale through the right nostril, close with the thumb, release the ring finger from the left side and exhale through the left nostril. This is one round of Alternate Nostril Breath.

- Perform 9 rounds of this alternating breath between the nostrils. Remember to always inhale through the same nostril you just exhaled through. Invite the breath to be smooth as silk and even without creating force or pressure. Notice how you feel, what you notice ...

exhale, inhale, switch

Exercise 14: Ujjayi Breathing

May be used to relieve overwhelming emotions in crowded places. It assists in blocking out incoming energies and assists in centering and calming. Inhale completely through to the lower belly and exhale out through the nose. Keep equal the length of each breath. Feel the breath flow over the back of your throat and allow the sound to calm you. It may sound like a distant ocean song calling you back to peace.

Place your hands over your ears as you practice these breathing techniques. What do you notice? How does the body feel? Internal hearing with the breath can feel and sound very healing. This is another way of connecting with your release and refill breathing patterns on a higher level.

With most of these breathing techniques, you can intensify the experience by playing with these two add-ons:

- Find a quiet space, slow your breath, close your eyes and visualize a person or place that you love. Imagine the smells and sounds of your special image. Let the peaceful feelings arise and replenish you.

- Place your hands over your ears as you practice some of these breathing techniques. It can take you into a deeper meditative state.

Select one or more of the Breathing Techniques and take notes: What do you notice? How does the body feel? Internal hearing with the breath can feel and sound very healing. This is another way of connecting with your release and refill breathing patterns on a higher level. What did you notice? How did this exercise feel?

18

The Seven Most Common Issues for Empaths:

Issue 1: Authenticity

We spend so much time blending with others that we often do not know who we are fully. We want people to be happy so we may not say much about ourselves and let people assume we feel the same way they do. This in fact is inauthentic. Find your tribe, so to speak. Find those who accept you just the way you are! You will find that it takes much more energy to hide who you are, and those that might not like you as you are would be healthier to release from your life anyway.

Exercise 15: Let Your Light Shine

Be as authentic as you can. Because empaths take on the energies of others, they often blend in. Consider googleing researching "raccoon totem" to learn about the lessons offered by the masked raccoon, which may assist you in removing your own masks. You will grow the courage and conviction to be exactly who you are. We often hide our unusual gifts, our different vibrations, for fear of rejection. In fact, we are incredibly gifted individuals when we are free to be who we are. Try not to hide away; be unashamed of your unique qualities.

What are some ways you can be more authentic in your own life?

Issue 2: Sacrificing Your Own Balance to Help Others

Needing to help others even if it is not good for you is all too often an empathic trait. We tend to feel the other person's need or unhappiness and we have a strong desire to make it better so that both of us feel better. Unfortunately, when we have not yet learned only to give from overflow and we have not realized that we need to say no even if it upsets the other person, we may end up soaking up the other person's drama. This cycle leaves our lives out of balance. If we keep giving our time, more time and energy than we really have to give, we end up unhappy. Sometimes we feel loved and valued for our keen listening abilities but we may find we end up being repeatedly used to resolve others' unhappiness and problems.

Exercise 16: Cultivate Space and Healthy Boundaries

- **Learn and Practice healthy boundaries**; allow sufficient space and time before saying yes.

  - "I will have to check my schedule later when I am at home. If you can email me the information, I will consider it." Often people will find someone else to fill their need and never follow through with contacting you about it again.

  - Put things back into their hands instead of you instantly taking things on, by switching the role of responsibility back to them.

  - Waiting to make a decision when you're not physically in the presence of the requester most often means making a more balanced decision if what is being asked is not something you would really want to do or have time for.

  - "No, I can't make it that day" You don't have to give a reason why, and often a short and sweet answer is better than trying to explain.

- **Practice tuning in to yourself**, disconnect from others' feelings and ask yourself, "Do I want to do this or am I really only doing it to make them happy?" If you can't yet tune in to yourself, disconnect eye contact or excuse yourself to the restroom then use that few minutes to evaluate how you are feeling when not in their presence.

- If you are often stressed, overwhelmed and anxious with an over-full life, ask yourself why you are taking on too much. Do you look for love, appreciation and acceptance by saying yes? Are you often mad at yourself after? If so, **your homework is to begin tuning into your needs first**.

- Realize that saving someone repeatedly does not allow them to grow and may harm them in the long run. Since this is the exact opposite of what you want, consider what it would look like if you took care of yourself instead.

What are some boundaries that you would like to cultivate going forward? Which ideas seem most fruitful to you at this point in your life?

_____

_____

_____

_____

_____

_____

_____

_____

_____

_____

_____

_____

_____

Issue 3: People Complaining to You Often and for Long Periods of Time. Being Caught in One-Way Conversations.

People experience healing in the presence of empaths. Part of the reason is that empaths are very good listeners and energetically give full attention. They are also very intuitive and often give the best advice available. It serves people well to take the empath's perspective into consideration because they are right most of the time. The issue is that this takes your valuable time and may turn into an unbalanced energy exchange. This means that often you walk away feeling drained or stressed out because it took up too much of your time. Then if you beat yourself up afterward for allowing someone to corner you and take your time or energy, the cost is even greater.

Exercise 17: Empathic Disengagement

- Refer to the "sacrificing of self to help others" section above.

- Disengage in eye contact – this helps with you to not be a captive audience. The eyes are the windows of the soul. Practice with someone – try to notice the difference in energy when you say "no" with direct eye contact and again when you say "no" when not looking directly at the person.

- State that you are "doing something else right now, thank you for starting a conversation but I need to do this right now."

- If you feel captured with no polite way out, **practice being impolite**. You might be surprised to find how good it feels.

What does it feel like to disengage energetically in a polite manner? In an "impolite" manner? Why are both important for an empath to master?

Issue 4: Feeling Out of Sorts, Spacy, Not Grounded

Due to the quantity of energetic input that many empaths absorb, it is easy to feel displaced from the earth and a bit lost at times. These exercises are important to do whenever additional grounding is needed to bring the empath back to a steady calm state.

Exercise 18: Energetic Taffy Pull

- Intend that your **hands are sticky** like the back of a post it note. Imagine that your hands stick to energy that is on or around you, sticking to that which is not of your highest good to keep. Stick the hands into the energy field around you and intend to pull it off. Notice how you feel afterwards, lighter, less encumbered.

- Intend that your hands pull subtle energy off the physical body. Extend your palms over the head and pull the energy down the body, down the legs, feet and into the earth for recycling. Next, cross the midline of the body beginning at the shoulder running across the hip and off the body to the earth. Repeat on the other side. Next, start with your shoulder and move down the arm with a flick, over and over. Then do the other arm. Repeat as often as it feels good to do so.

- Pull off energy or a negative emotion from the body wherever it feels appropriate to do so.

- Standing tall, arms at your sides with finger tips pointing down. Intend that all unhelpful energy run from the body down the arms into the ground. Nothing will come off that you need, this will only remove that which drags you down.

When do you most need to do an Energetic Taffy Pull? What people, places, or events come to mind?

Issue 5: Experiencing Paranormal Activity in Your Life

The lack of true understanding toward paranormal events may cause fear, anxiety and suppression of such abilities. These abilities are natural, not a coincidence or a magical spell. Each empath is unique, some will recognize this issue and some will not.

Exercise 19: Embrace Multidimensional Reality

- Think about and remember times where there were unexplained synchronicities in your life, unexplainable knowing.

- Instead of fear, when something happens, consider thinking along the lines of "well isn't that interesting?" or "amazing?" or "what are the odds?"

- Step away from the fear-based teachings of your past. Trust your intuition. Trust your divine ways of knowing as an empathic gift. Let go of cultural fear conditioning and embrace the true nature of life as an empath.

- Find your tribe, so to speak. Connect with other people that understand these situations.

Can you describe a synchronistic event in your life that felt like it was perhaps paranormal? How did you react? How did those close to you react to your sensitivities? How has your cultural, economic, or religious programming shaped your perception of such gifts? How could you improve your experience of these gifts?

Issue 6: Not Recognizing Energy

. Sometimes we become disconnected from our ability to discern energy. Being able to feel and move energy is something we should regularly cultivate in order to enjoy all the fruits of our empathic blessings. Try this exercise to reconnect with the feelings of auric energy.

Exercise 20: Pouring Energy Ball

- Rubbing the hands together briskly, bring in the warmth and then visualize, imagine or feel a small ball of energy forming.
  - Stay with it, can you make it bigger?
  - What does it feel like?

- Intend to pour energy from one hand to the next.
  - Imagine pouring sand from one hand slowly into the other and back several times,
  - Can you imagine it? Can you feel it?

- Scan someone's energy with both hands, palms facing them.
  - Now try it with the left hand, then the right.
  - Do you notice changes as you go from head to toe slowly?

Have you ever felt disconnected from your energetic gifts? How did it feel to move the energy between your palms? Can you envision this energy as a loving supportive light?

"To know thyself is the beginning of wisdom."

—Socrates

"The implications of recognizing, first, that subtle energetic bodies fill and surround all life, and second, that many of us unknowingly allow such energies to influence our moods and physical bodies, have breathtaking repercussions for our health and well being.

If we learn how to properly strengthen our energetic boundaries, and thereby our empathic immune system, as April carefully and thoroughly details in this book, we free ourselves from unnecessary and potentially harmful burdens of the mind, body, and soul, all of which never belonged to us in the first place. It does not require a stretch of the imagination to envision the vast, profound, and multifarious benefits of life as an empath [people with empathic abilities are often referred to as an empath], unburdened by the heavy moods (emotional accumulations), opinions, and even medical problems we have laid upon ourselves without conscious recognition.

In Healing for Empaths, April gives us the tools we need to reclaim the agency we did not even realize we had given away. With our power restored, we learn that we get to choose what enters our bodies and souls—that we have profound power over our own lives.

As a physician, I can only imagine the [incredible] health benefits we will see [that may occur] when empaths begin taking their power back and fortifying their energetic boundaries with the techniques April has developed. With the enhanced empathic immune system, over-stimulated children will calm, overwhelmed adults will find peace, and many more will correct imbalances that lead to serious illness, not to mention the benefit of acquiring a deeper understanding of one's own inner workings.

With April's guidance, we can learn to harness the untapped potential of whatever our unique form of empathy empowers us with. We may Ram, Uam, Ham, to intuit the reason for a loved one's distress, and support him with the comfort and healing that deep understanding provides. We may be able to recognize at some preverbal level exactly what a dying plant needs to thrive—or even borrow another's skill at shaping pottery for an afternoon. The possibilities are limitless.

The book you hold in your hands is a profoundly powerful one. May it guide you to greater understanding of your soul and a resonant peace in your heart."

Dr. Robert Gerber

Your life is now forever changed.

By using the tools in this book to increase awareness of and tuning in to subtle energies, empaths are provided the keys to unlocking healing processes that build their energetic immune systems bringing not only greater health and vitality but also better connect them to their souls purposes.

It is a time of transformation away from darkness and fear into a place of love, light, joy, and fun.

If you are looking for additional support in maintaining your flow of love and joy, learn more April´s "365 Self-Love" Program and the "Integrated Healing for Empaths" Program at http://aprilwalker.com

"I signed up for the "Integrated Healing for Empaths" Program because I wanted to learn the different types of Empaths that exist and how to protect myself, my daughter and my family. Growing up I knew I had special abilities, but I did not know what they were or why. Boy am I glad that I did take this program!! I always feel so comfortable with April due to her kind demeanor and quirky sense of humor! I learned many tools to cleanse my home; my body, mind and spirit; my past and my whole family! This program is EXACTLY what I needed to understand who I am! I really appreciated April added the part about Empathic Children!! This was a wealth of information for me as a parent of an Empath teen. It really helped me make sense of the confusing world my daughter and I lived in all these years. All that April explained was exactly what my daughter had gone through as a toddler, child and now young adult. It all makes sense now! She and I learned so much together and I have to admit, this class has helped us grow closer as we have something very special in common and we both love and appreciate our gifts.

This program is a must! It is a necessary tool to understand what it is to be an Empath and how to deal with the everyday issues and feelings that we go through, meet other Empaths, and most importantly, how to protect yourself and remain balanced in our world of muggles! LOL. I now feel so much more confident in who I am and more confident on how to protect myself and my daughter.

I feel lighter, vibrant and fabulous!

I JUST LOVED THIS CLASS!!

Olga P, CA

For more information, visit: www. aprilwalker.com/empath

Made in the USA
Middletown, DE
27 March 2020